AF710451

Free to Care

Therapy for the Whole Family of Concerned Persons

TERENCE WILLIAMS

HAZELDEN
BOX 176
CENTER CITY, MINNESOTA 55012

Sixth Printing, March, 1980

Copyright © 1975
Hazelden Foundation

ISBN: 0-89486-050-X

Printed in the United States of America

In this first of the Hazelden pamphlets for concerned persons, we would like to offer some ideas that we at Hazelden have about what seems to happen to people who are emotionally involved with addicts and about what these people can do to save themselves. Bear with us, will you please, when we use the term *addict* to refer to chemically dependent people, people who are harmfully dependent on drugs, any and all drugs, including alcohol, the most common drug of abuse in our culture. And let's define as *family* everyone who knows and cares about an addict. We would like to discuss why we think it is important to provide therapy for the whole family of concerned persons—for the immediate family, and for the friends and neighbors, and for employers of addicts—even if the addict refuses to be involved in the therapy. We would like to offer our message of hope for those who care.

We hear a lot these days about the death of the family as an institution, about how the traditional family system is increasingly unable to cope with the demands for growth and change in contemporary society. Maybe the family is changing its style, maybe the family is no longer the socio-economic basis for the traditional community, but a family of some kind—however broadly we define it—is an emotional survival system, something that each of us is involved with, in one form or another. Certainly every addict has a survival system that includes other people, and addiction is, indeed, a family disease. According to experts, every addict has a significant and direct impact on the lives of several other people.

The Family's Own Addiction

What happens to these people, to these concerned persons, when one or more members of the emotional survival system become addicted to alcohol or other drugs? Why do we call chemical addiction a family disease? We think that as a chemical addiction becomes more and more apparent, it becomes more and more important in the life of the family. In some terrible way, the family's struggle to control the addict's behavior or somehow to escape from the consequences of his behavior begins to govern the family's whole life-style. As the family struggles to cope, typically they become bound up in a destructive pattern of recurring, predictably bad situations. Just as the addict himself suffers, they suffer deeply, but they can't seem to bring about any kind of change in their lives. It is our observation that concerned persons become addicted to the addict in much the same way he is addicted to drugs.

The real tragedy of addiction, it seems to us, is that the addict eventually reaches a point at which he begins to feel bad about himself, even though he may put a lot of effort into masking his bad feelings. Every addict is aware, when he is really hooked, that drugs and/or alcohol are more important in his life than family, or job, or health—aware that the drug experience is *too* important. At the same time, a really fantastic denial system offers him a false awareness that the next time things will be different, that he can control his drug use. Inevitably, he fails again, and failure after failure damages his feelings of self-worth. He begins to feel helpless and worthless. It seems that something a lot like this also happens to the people who are emotionally involved with addicts.

As the addict becomes more dependent upon his drug, the family puts more energy into coping with the situation, and coping becomes a central part of their lives: they anticipate the drinking and other drug use, they bear with it somehow while it goes on, and they adjust in order to absorb the harmful consequences as each cycle ends. They know, in their hearts, that they cannot change the addict. At some level, they actually are aware of this. At the same time, something quite like the addict's denial system tells them that they can help the addict, that they can remedy the situation, if they just hold on, that things will be different—next time. When the cycle inevitably repeats itself, the family of concerned persons suffers. Those people whose own sense of emotional well-being is deeply dependent upon the addict and his behavior begin to feel helpless, to feel worthless, just as he does. It is almost as if the people who are concerned about addicts become addicted themselves in proportion to the depth of their concern. And everyone in the family of the addict becomes involved in a no-win game called "Next Time It Will Be Different."

When concerned persons become hooked, they unwittingly accept the role of enabler for the addict. Another term to describe this role is hurt—or angry—or frightened—caretaker for the addict. These family members sometimes become saviors: a healthy, kind and loving part of them says that they have the responsibility to save the addict ("I know I am a capable person, and I know I can help—if I can just find the answers."); or they become partners, drinking with the addict, trying to join him in his game and to win him over to some reasonable behavior this way ("Right now he needs me, and we are going to stick together until we have this licked."); or they become victims, the martyrs, and—suffering already from a low self-concept—they assume the self-defeating role of people whose mission in life is to suffer ("It's my duty as a wife, husband, parent . . . I know things will be better some day."); or they become tough guys, trying vainly to force the addict into changing his behavior ("What this kid needs is some military therapy, two years in the service! They'll straighten him out!"). Concerned persons will play one or more of these roles at one time or another; or one of the roles will be their way of relating to the addict. In some way, however, they establish themselves as being responsible for the addict. In each of these roles, there is the implicit assumption that the concerned persons can somehow change the addict, and it is this assumption, together with the addict's defiance, that keeps the game going.

Each role feeds the addict's resistance to change; he doesn't really need to change, in any event, because the family keeps telling him—through their efforts to fix him—that they will take responsibility for him. The family doesn't know this, however, and to suggest that they are partners in the addiction, that they too are hooked, and that their enabling behavior is important in maintaining the drug and alcohol use, can cause them to feel more guilty than they already do feel, can reinforce the delusion they already have that somehow they have caused the drinking and other drug use. Describing their involvement in the addictive process can also make them feel more helpless, more frustrated, and more full of self-pity than they are already.

Gaining Awareness

It seems to us that the only way to change the sick family system when the whole thing finally becomes unbearable is to help the concerned persons to understand the system and to see their roles in it, to help them look at their own addiction to the addict. It is only with understanding that each family member can take responsibility for his part in the system.

What we do is make every effort we can to respect the family's situation—to understand it and to reassure the family that it is totally reasonable. We try to feel how important the addictive relationships are for the family—to respect the family truly and to look at it without judging it; to appreciate the family. Then together we try to examine the relationships. The family systems approach of such family therapists as Murray Bowen, Don Jackson, Jay Haley, Carl Whitaker, Virginia Satir and others is helpful in discussing the enabling role in a non-judgmental way, and this approach parallels the A.A. and Al-Anon philosophy.

In a recent article, "A Family Systems Approach To Alcoholism" (*Addictions:* Summer 1974), Murray Bowen says, "In systems theory the focus is on the functional facts of relationships, on what happens, how it happens, where it happens, insofar as such observations are based on facts. It carefully avoids man's preoccupation with *why it happens.*" Bowen goes on to say, "From a systems viewpoint, alcoholism is one of the common human dysfunctions. As a dysfunction it exists in the context of an imbalance in functioning of the total family system. From a theoretical viewpoint every important family member plays a part in the dysfunction of the dysfunctional member. This theory provides a way for conceptualizing the *part* each member plays. Therapy is directed at the family member or family members with the most resourcefulness, who have the most potential for modifying their own function. When it is possible to modify the family relationship system the alcoholic dysfunction improves even though the dysfunctional one may not have been part of the therapy."

We want to qualify what Bowen says: the alcoholic dysfunction may "improve" for the separate family members and the alcoholic may then decide to take responsibility for his own behavior; but there is no assurance of this: the alcoholic may very well move on to find another caretaker, and this is frequently what happens. The important point that Bowen makes is that the concerned persons can interrupt the destructive cycle of family-wide emotional addiction, even if the addict continues to use alcohol and other drugs. They can, if they are willing, give up their caretaker roles and can begin their own emotional growth, quite apart from the addict. If they are able to give up their roles in the sick family system, they also by this action do all they are able to do in freeing the addict to grow too. He may not accept this freedom to grow—but he may.

Letting Go

If the family does not feel blamed, if their self-hatred and frustration are not fed by the therapist as they examine the dysfunctional family system, they are sometimes ready to see that they must step out of their enabling roles, their caretaker roles. They may be willing to deal with their own addictive relationships. The big problem is to help the family work through the process of letting go, freeing themselves from something that has become a very important part of their lives. If the concerned persons, the caretakers, are willing to face the uncertainty, the adventure in living, that marks the end of their sick roles in the sick family systems, therapy can help them with the process of grieving that necessarily accompanies the end of their old relationships.

Therapy cannot help much, it seems to us, in persuading people to give up addictive caretaker relationships when they still believe that controls are possible alternatives. Typically, these are people who believe that A.A. or therapists or rehabilitation centers can cure the addict and return him or her safe and sound to the same family system. But therapy can help, we think, when the caretakers have already decided they must end the sick relationship but cannot figure out how to do it. We can help when they are willing to begin growing. We can help when they are still afraid they have only two equally unacceptable alternatives: 1) to go on putting up with the crazy behavior of the addict, or 2) to divorce the addict, kick him out of the house, or otherwise remove him from their lives. We can help them to see that there is a third way, another alternative. This third way involves coming to terms with the fact that no one can change other people, that caretaking does not cause healthy change in anyone.

The end of the caretaking relationship is the end of this very important part of the lives of concerned persons. It is the death of a relationship, a loss. Just think of the time and the emotional energy that concerned persons spend trying to do something constructive about the problem of addiction. Even if all this experience has been painful and frustrating, it has become a vital part of the whole family's life-style, and giving up the old role, it is important to realize, will necessarily involve a great deal of sadness.

In what may seem an unlikely way to discuss recovery and growth, we would like to say something about "grief work," about the process of reaching acceptance of the end of relationships, about accepting losses. One of the best discussions of this subject is a book by Elisabeth Kübler-Ross, a psychiatrist who worked for some time with terminally ill patients in hospitals. *On Death and Dying* (New York, Macmillan, 1969) is her study of how people are able to accept death, the end of all relationships. The stages that she describes seem to be something that people we work with can use to conceptualize the death of their sick relationships with addicts. Try to see if any of this fits your own experience.

The Denial Stage

The first stage in the process of moving toward acceptance of death is *denial*. People who are sick can and often will deny that they are sick, will refuse to accept a doctor's diagnosis. This is, after all, a pretty natural thing for us to do. In related ways, we can deny that we need glasses by simply putting off the business of having our eyes checked. We can deny that we need to have dental work done by avoiding the dentist. And so forth. The person who is emotionally involved with an addict denies that he cannot somehow control the situation, usually by denying that he or she is even trying to do that. Some people, even in the groups we work with in a treatment center, will in fact deny that the addict spouse or child or parent or friend is an addict—will deny that there really is a problem. Others will retreat to this position if the process of ending the sick relationship seems too painful and difficult. Denial seems to derive from the concerned person's fear—fear of somehow betraying the addict by admitting what is happening, or fear of the therapy process itself. Our goal in working with people who are in the denial stage is to help them feel safe enough to look at what is actually happening in the family's life.

The Anger Stage

The next stage a dying person must work through in attempting to accept the fact of his impending death is *anger*. When they can no longer deny their illness, terminally ill patients experience feelings of anger and self-pity. "My God, why is this happening to me?" "What have I done to deserve this fate?" "Why? Why? Why?" they keep asking. Concerned persons who have passed through the stage of denial, who have admitted that they have been trying to fix the addict and that their efforts have all failed, are often filled with similar feelings of anger and self-pity. They are angry at the addict, at themselves, at life itself, because they are frustrated at every turn. All their efforts have failed, and angrily they will file for divorce or kick the child out of the house or run away themselves. Enraged, they murder! Anger and some kind of crazy energy govern their lives. Or else they are locked in a smoldering kind of passive-aggressive hostility. Divorce, enforced separation, suicide, murder, or endless grinding resentment are products of this kind of situation—unless these people find some kind of relief. Our goal here with concerned persons is to help them to own their own anger, to recognize and deal with their own feelings. They are letting the addict control them. They are lost in their own addiction. Often a lot of progress can be made when people realize how specifically they let themselves be controlled by the addict, how their whole relationship is loaded with self-fulfilling prophecies and disappointments. They can sometimes see how letting go can permit them to have again the choice of caring . . .

The Bargaining Stage

As the dying person faces his death, he often passes through a stage of *bargaining*—trying to make a deal with the doctor or with God. He pleads for just one more day, just one more springtime, just one more visit with his family—just one more chance. When concerned persons see how futile and destructive their anger is, how pointless their self-pity, they too are prone to bargain. "I am a parent, after all, and a parent has to exercise some control!" "Do you mean we just have to let him die?" "Isn't there something we can do?" But the real bargaining point for the contemporary, well-informed caretaker has to do with rehabilitation programs: "How do we go about getting him (her) into treatment?" "What are commitment proceedings and how do they work?" "What is the best rehabilitation center?" Our goal in working with these people is to help them let go entirely, to feel their powerlessness to change another person, to move on to the next stage in their grief work. Eventually, when they realize that commitment can be accomplished only for their own sake, not for the addict's sake, they can turn that way if they want to.

The Depression Stage

Elisabeth Kübler-Ross says that when dying people can no longer deny their illness, when their anger does them no good and when bargaining proves futile, they endure a period of depression. In a hospital, depressed people facing death isolate themselves. They refuse to receive visitors, refuse to eat, refuse the comfort that others offer them. They cry—quietly, as they come to a full awareness of their powerlessness. This is Step One in Al-Anon and A.A. Concerned persons who finally learn to know that they are powerless to change the addict will cry too, and sometimes they refuse to move on to the last stage of grief work. People who are locked in depression are usually more resistant to therapy than others. Sometimes they will continue to grieve for years. The goal of therapy with these people is to help them to keep working, to encourage them to be aware of their feelings, to understand them and to pass through them into the final stage of their grief work—*acceptance*.

The Acceptance Stage

In Al-Anon and A.A., some kind of peace of mind is available to people who are able to take the first three steps. The first step is "We admitted we were powerless over alcohol—that our lives had become unmanageable." Concerned persons must realize their powerlessness over the alcoholic, the addict. The Second Step: "Came to believe that a Power greater than ourselves could restore us to sanity." And the Third Step: "Made a decision to turn our will and our lives over to the care of God as we understood Him." These are the stages that the addict must pass through as he learns to accept the death of his relationship with alcohol and other drugs. They are the stages that concerned persons work through as they accept the death of their caretaker roles. They are almost like a summary of the stages that Kübler-Ross describes in her study of how people are able to accept death. We all have the God-given ability to accept the end of our lives with peace and dignity.

Being Free to Care

Our message of hope is that concerned persons can learn how to escape from their addictive relationships with addicts with this same kind of peace and dignity and to build healthy lives for themselves. They can learn to be comfortable in their awareness that they are unable to change the addict. At this point they are able to detach emotionally from the addict's problem. They are free to give the problem back to the addict. They can now love the addict again, care *about* him and not care *for* him—understand him, without internalizing the problem if the addict uses drugs again or relapses by drinking, and without taking credit for the whole process if the addict decides to take responsibility for his own feelings again, and for his own behavior. They can be free to care.

Hazelden

Listed here are other publications you'll find interesting written by Terence Williams, the supervisor of the Family Program at Hazelden.

Recovery for the Whole Family

by Harold A. Swift, A.C.S.W. and Terence Williams, M.A.

Initial recovery is only a single battle in the war for the alcoholic and the family. Includes vivid, realistic descriptions of the obstacles in store for the family while it seeks for itself the most happiness possible.

order #1409

Taking Stock (a personal inventory)

by Harold Swift, A.C.S.W. and Terence Williams, M.A.

Gentle and yet probing are the guidelines offered in this Fourth Step inventory. Although written specifically for persons recovering with the help of Al-Anon, it will appeal to all people who need the Twelve Step Program.

Harold A. Swift is the Administrator of Hazelden Foundation and Terence Williams is supervisor of the Family Program at Hazelden.

order #1433

To order any of these call one of our Educational Services Outreach Representatives.

Hazelden
Educational Services

Box 176, Center City, MN 55012
(800) 328-9288 (T...
(612...
(612...

13
Free to Care: -ot demaris
50314477
089486050X - Fast Track ...
ree to Care: Therapy for t...
t Oriana ¦ -
975 ¦ pamphlet

1292 — 15M